SP

ESSENTIAL POETS SERIES 112

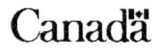

Canada

Guernica Editions Inc. acknowledges support of The Canada Council for the Arts.
Guernica Editions Inc. acknowledges support from the Ontario Arts Council.
Guernica Editions Inc. acknowledges the financial support of the Government of Canada
through the Book Publishing Industry Development Program (BPIDP).

ROBIN BLACKBURN

IN GREEN

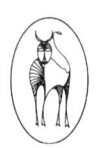

GUERNICA
TORONTO·BUFFALO·LANCASTER (U.K.)
2002

Copyright © 2002, by Robin Blackburn and Guernica Editions Inc.
All rights reserved. The use of any part of this publication, reproduced,
transmitted in any form or by any means, electronic, mechanical,
photocopying, recording or otherwise stored in a retrieval system, without
the prior consent of the publisher is an infringement of the copyright law.

Antonio D'Alfonso, editor
Guernica Editions Inc.
P.O. Box 117, Station P, Toronto (ON), Canada M5S 2S6
2250 Military Road, Tonawanda, N.Y. 14150-6000 U.S.A.
Gazelle, Falcon House, Queen Square, Lancaster LA1 1RN U.K.

First edition.
Typeset by Selina.
Printed in Canada.

Legal Deposit – First Quarter
National Library of Canada
Library of Congress Catalog Card Number: 2002102764

National Library of Canada Cataloguing in Publication Data
Blackburn, Robin
In green
(Essential poets series ; 112)
ISBN 1-55071-154-7
I. Title. II. Series.
PS8553.L3223I6   2002   C811'.6   C2002-900512-4
PR9199.4.B53I6   2002

Contents

Acknowledgements	6
Egg	9
With Baby	10
Story Time	11
Stumps and Roots	13
Night	15
1977: Fitting	17
1899: Beginning, Finishing	19
Tempest	21
Departures	22
Wedding Gift	25
Letters	26
Woman and Wolf	27
Theories	30
Harvest	31
Fold	32
Seth	33
Morning Glories	47
Visitors	48
Can't	50
Her Horses	51
Ghosts	52
Split in the Round	53
Strange Embers	54
Keeping Tabs	56
Reality Bites	58
Nymph	59
On the Beach with My Daughter	62
Fabric	63
Lines	66
In Green	67

Acknowledgements

Some of these poems have appeared in the *Hart House Review*, *Pagitica*, and *Room of One's Own*. Thanks go to Antonio D'Alfonso, Halli Villegas, Julie Roorda, Sue Bowness, John O'Neill, John Barton, Stephanie Bolster, Bruce Meyer, The Taddlecreek Summer Writers' Workshop, and Austin Clarke. "Fabric" is for Jacinthe Roy, and many dear friends. I would like to thank my family for the inspiration.

For my family

Egg

She was poised on something whole
wanting to keep it contained beneath her
forever heating it and fueled by it
in a nest she made from her own hair.

But it cracked.

It was meant to
though the avian logic defies.

Her tears seep through fissures in the shell –
sting the life inside
as it moves
unrevealed.

And she squats furious
above the shifting plates
too sharp to touch
too fragile to leave
in the violence of beginnings.

With Baby

I look around us at this place
at the houses of relations –
people planted deep,
foundations.

I look at trees which I have called old
and keys,
at signs that tell me the trails below
the ones we follow
with you ever watching
as the scenes behind us change.
This pattern of disappearances is your first.

I push you in your carriage
under a canopy of yellow leaves
past the curling lips of roses:
contours of unvoiced departure.

You smile at the detail you trust
and sights are altered.

One day
you will view another landscape.
I have not seen its paths.
Like others already
I move beneath them.

Story Time

My daughter insists that I read to her each night.

She demands to know the tale of Vasalisa
who moved through her dark world
to an old woman's house of bone and light.

There is Persephone
who ripped white flowers from the earth
and herself was torn the other way –
her mother, wild,
forcing winters to stop the growing.

I tell of Old Mother Swan
seeking Earthquake
who married off her daughters for meat
and a dry lodge roof.

Mother Hölle is the favorite,
about the girl with bleeding fingers
who fell through a well into a world
where she was saved
by listening.

My neck is gripped for several seconds,
released
by a small arm.

Covers are secured
eyes flash
hair is smoothed across the forehead.

We leave a light on in the corner
as she finishes our story with the same words every time:

"Where are you going to be?"

Stumps and Roots

Something makes me step back
over the raised doorsills of time.

I step
without stumbling,
careful not to let others hear,
avoid rusty nails
strangers
poison fruit.

I shrink
to the size of an unpricked finger,
move cautiously over the pages
in our fairy tale collection.

Here is a picture of the girl with her basket.
How can I tell my daughter, who I read to,
that the child we see on the page is me?

Walk anyway
past stumps and roots
to where parents lose their young
in shadows
and a bear could snap a neck
like wood.

Crawl
into the house
too snug
for my skin.
Bones pressed tight
in lath and plaster swaddling.

My ancestor draws me
calls me to reach in
to where each small detail looms.
Her life played out in whispers here,
a forest warning.

In childhood we are closest
to the ghosts that formed us.

I must go back to know better
where I came from.
No need to mark the trees
with the tip of a silver knife.

I recognize the way.

Night

I am warm
tightly covered
but she comes.

Hear the drag of heavy feet
and her cane tap.

I close my eyes pretending
to sleep.
Blankets are smoothed
around my feet
and over my fists she pulls
the comforter.

I lie like a stone.

Hear her climb
into the bed across
and the limping stops.

My grandma curls
into memory
as I roll the other way

imagining

the old
sleep like coral
secret animals of the deep
who rise and fall
with the sway of hidden currents.

She should not know how I fear the sea.

I will open my eyes
after she has settled
into the long night.

1977: Fitting

Because we begged her
she pulls the dress from its dry box
and we lay it out.
Its wrinkles compel me
like the lines on my palm.
I am not sure how to read them.

On the dress is an astonishment of hooks.

Floorboards creak
as my grandmother withdraws
and my cousin and I take turns
at fitting.
Arms into arms.
Eager fingers press metal
through the old eyes that hold.

The fabric grips me.

From its burial place in a cabinet drawer
I pull the photograph of the woman
who once wore this dress.
Fall Fair, 1908.
My ancestor signed in black
before she vanished,
traveling only through blood now.

I search for patterns in the sepia,
veins along the skirt and petals
which curl out and up the angles of my body . . .

A print of orange blooms
spreads across me and I blaze
to the mirror
in a sudden garden –
turning in the weight,
opening in the full cloth:
"My hair is like hers!" I call to my cousin,
"Look at my eyes!"

The room is silent.

Bent fingers seize at the clasps on my throat
undo them

and I am pulled from silken tiger lilies
like a jaw-stunned bird.

My grandmother folds her mother's dress
back into its box.
Shakes her head.
"Her hair was different."
Her hands smooth along the crease lines.

1899: Beginning, Finishing

Another sepia photograph shows
a young woman's room in Ithaca, New York.
Great-grandmother stayed there,
her finishing school before marriage.
Beginning or finishing?

She will leave to marry the farmer who waits
and one day will name my grandma
after the lady of that New York house,
the one who says, "Don't go."

In the photo there is a couch with fringe
and leaves
embroidered on pillow sleeves.
A banjo is propped against a wall
where other pictures hang – her sketches.
Letters home wait to be sent.

The young woman is missing from the picture
though everywhere are her decisions:
the angle of the table
the pattern on the throw
the lamp in the window beside the bowl of apples.

Ghost of a stillborn child.

Years later people said the farmer's house
lacked a woman's touch.

My grandma shut her ears.

Tempest

The child fixes her expression,
mending a dropped china cup.
If she holds the pieces still enough
the cracks won't show.
There is a glow
from the face of this girl.
Glaze
won't interrupt.
She remains, calm mill water,
while adult words crash
not rippling her surface.
She waits for the storm to be over.
Interior whirlpools start out small
hold a child in place
where she sits
tall.

Departures

I
In the garden
hands like morning glories
grip a child's white shoulders
for the last time.

The woman wears traveling clothes.

What feather will her daughter later find
in the dirt?
Heat makes the skin damp
under her heavy dress.

What green veins will be crushed
on the road out past a South Durham farm?

The child stays behind,
spins, "Look at me, Mama, I'm a windmill,"

as the wagon moves
and the earth twirls
and the waving woman goes.

Empty wagon
on the still field
marks time.

Inside the house
the woman's desk is locked
like Pharaoh's tomb.
Through the years men will strike
their matches on it.

Outside a windmill turns,
silent.

II
She keeps her mother's life a secret.

Seeds are blown on the wind
to escape the shadow
of the parent plant.
Words carry —
taunt *canker-worms on budding hearts*
and *hereditary degeneration*.
Spelled out in blight,
locked away in wood.

She keeps her mother's life a secret.

A child stops spinning
runs straight along a dirt road
chased by voices,
the calls of crows.

Moves away from that early garden.
Runs so hard she breaks
and blooms without regret
into the full rose
elsewhere
watching us appear and scatter.

Her legs never work right again;
she feels that she's come far enough.

III
She never runs from anything.

Roots here
at each place called home
where we find her.

This mother's love
a stubborn flower
sustains itself, ungardened
along the roadsides even now.

Before she dies
my grandmother asks to be buried deep
so a child alone
may find a place with her.

Wedding Gift

My father hauls the desk,
a relic wedding gift
from a farm on the Eleventh Range.

They whip along highways
wind-beaten through two provinces
to the refinisher
who holds it fleetingly in acid hands
and sends it on –
my Toronto door blown open.

My father explains how they did their best
to eliminate strike marks
and other scratches on the surface of the boards.

"The grain has come up quite nicely," he says.

Keys once lost
have been replaced.

Doctors' letters locked inside
pronounced the bride's fate years ago:
the necessity of her early parting
contradicted the craftsman's symmetry.
Stark words have been removed

before the wooden legs are carried
across my threshold.

Letters

Asking my father for the letters that were shut away
plays out a family
song of dread.

I am aware, as I make the call,
of how he might respond.
Numerous throat clearings,
shovels full of earth.

In my mind
the two of us stand
eye to eye,
spade to spade,
silhouettes
on an unnamed field.

He knows that when he leaves I will stay,
that where he has filled
I will dig.

There is respect in the turning of a back
and trust in walking,
the sound of metal
hitting objects
underground.

Woman and Wolf

The animal must have been tied
deep inside her
wrapped sticky wet
around her bones
concealed
from all who stared
wondering
just how exactly she was marked.

Claws everywhere
were disguised
by the smiles she learned
as a child,
one of ten
at a diningroom table.

Her lace collar was tight
around the beating tail.
She thought it was her heart.

"My goodness,"
she said one day at last,
"I seem to have swallowed a wolf."

The woodcutter came into the wrong story.
Slit the woman with a knife he used
for carving chairs.

She lay there embarrassed by her entrails
which a lady wasn't supposed to show —
apologized for the matted fur
the second heart beat
and a howl
she was sure she didn't eat on purpose.

The man kept slicing.

She lay wide open
amidst the table settings,
silver serving trays,
turnips and spoon
beside her left ear.
Down alongside her right hip
was the little gravy boat
that had sailed with the family
from that port in Annan
all those years ago

before the woman and wolf were born
right here in this farm house
with its rose-covered carpets.

The other offspring cowered.
Checked themselves for lupine tendencies.

"Hold her ankles while I pull it out,"
said the woodcutter.
The father held one ankle,
the husband held the other,

and beside her right ear
with the plate of boiled carrots
her mother must have said,
"Hold still,"
because she was very still
compared to the animal
scuttling out
who left
its bloody paw prints on the roses.

Theories

Hysterectomy was said to fix a woman's problems,
cheer her up
settle her down.

In 1910 there was no replacement therapy.
Estrogen was a word in a foreign language,
the endocrine system
an uncharted sea.
After being ripped apart
a person feels uneasy.

Hysteria follows hysterectomy in the dictionary.
Not all cuts are by the knife.

There were a lot of Latin names
coming over on ships and spreading.
Theories raised in the labs of Europe
grew wild at roadside hospitals;
it was said nothing much could be done.
Depression was a moral illness,
field guides were scarce.
Tending minds forced questions of flower or weed:
matters of perspective.
Certain varieties found conditions rough.

Harvest

I discover she was exiled
for sadness
and I wonder if she chose her ride.
Each time her husband came to visit her
she cried
and they sent a letter after him.
One day he stopped.
Went back to ploughs
that were easier to pull
than her heart behind him.

The source of her pain
remains
undocumented.
I could search through all the pages
and never find her sorrow spelled in words.

Somewhere the woman's heart
found a place to hide
from all who had marked it.
Furrows scored deep
in the silent land of muscle
she harvested
alone.

Fold

While he was growing
he did not know his grandmother
was alive in the Verdun asylum.

White face behind storm window glass
by the lamp and watching
where fields had been.

One day he was surprised by his mother's voice,
called to be a child again
beside a stranger's casket.

Mother of the mother:
returned after fifty years
to this unexpected gathering.

I imagine sprays of roses
near her driftwood hands
and people studying her
for traces
of themselves.

She was folded quickly into the ground,
a letter into a dark drawer.

I was born aware of the lines.

Seth

I *Synapses, Synopsis*

Osiris
killed twice by his brother Seth
was reborn a god –
resurrected by Isis
who knew that death by shadow
is a necessary murder,
and the words, "You will betray me,"
are words of love in some families.

Seth also learned about love.

II *Early Years*

Wrench of light
turned his legs to twisting blades
inside the cow.

She shivered
as he ripped her open.
He did not like tight spaces.
It was nothing personal.

Mangled ureters,
strings of hacked canal
became his hurricane out.

Chaos was born with teeth.
He chewed his own chord
and puked,
landed on the red mat
that was his food bag in confinement.

Nut, his mother, would dye a dress in his residue
and wear it to signal storms.

Seth was her child.

She scooped him in the jelly of his arrival,
licked his salt
and soothed his cares.
He nestled under a swollen teat,
sighed "Mama" and hunkered down.

Seth learned to walk early, as the others would,
to bring her rye-and-gingerales.
Her eyes glazed over
and she would say in some ways he was an easy child.

Seth weaned himself from the lacerated utters,
licked his chops and grinned.

He learned to drive his earth-god dad's Impala
and to hunt his own food
between the Texacos and Coffee Times
of the north-east Delta.

"Roadkill, cigarettes, and women."

Seth waxed oracular to his brother Osiris,
and to the scrawny sister Nephthys,
who would only ever birth a dog.

All that
when he brought his laundry home on weekends
for the cow who wore red linen,

who always said that she was glad to see him,
and he her, as he pulled his knife
and tossed it —
performing tricks with his sister Isis.

It was she who marked him.
Drove him crazy when she caught it in her teeth.

III *Stall*

So crazy
he stopped driving.

He sat by the Nile with the unkilled voles
nattering at his ankles.

Seth screwed holes in the bank
with a sharpened river stick and lost

his appetite. Stopped imagining
tread marks glistening

after the weight of four-by-fours
and the old taste of gravel in his lunch.

What was the point?

At night he stopped sleeping,
paced the Delta in a Camel cloud:

tar sucked deep. Breasts.
He only wanted hers.

Seth became the road.

Once, when he did nod off, he dreamed
of blackened underbelly

the hot weight and throb of radials coming down on him
and woke up tasting metal.

Isis returned his knife.
She knew he'd need to cut out for a while.

IV *Mysteries*

Being the goddess of knowledge wasn't easy.
Past Seth's flaws, the scorch marks she could see,
Isis also saw into him where his blood pulsed green
and promising.

Maybe it was just that she liked his dark hair,
or the way his lips curled when he grinned at her.

Even Isis wasn't sure where attractions came from
or where they went.
That information had been withheld from sky and earth,
so she went to water seeking answers
but only saw her own reflection
distorted
in the circles of her tears.

By the river's edge
in the cool clay
she stood on the holes that spelled her name.

V *Repairs*

She was tired
of putting it all back together.

Her marriage,
the severed bones she puzzled.

Bits of tooth, hair, skin,
rage, regret, in different piles.

This time she would glue him, she always said.
Make a backing.

Pieces went missing
and she had to search the carpets.

She traced a hole where passion was
on a cardboard box

cut carefully
and colored it the best she could.

VI *Trip*

Again Seth drove.

Wind beat through the windows of his black car
stalking eye sockets
ears and open mouth
until his skin bled
and sand
sprayed out like surf
under the spinning wheels.
For the first time Seth cried.

The red face
and grit rivulets in the rear-view mirror
were a mystery to him.

He drove
until the hood flew up.
Seth's tires burned on unknown lands
and sparks ignited

until the Impala was a ball of flame
busting out of landscape.

He gripped the handle in a furious flourish,
ripped the door off
and jumped –
rolled through cliff and catapult
for the first time feeling
the freshness of air
caressed and careening down
to sea:
a larger fact of water than he had ever known.

Depth.

For a while the cold was a relief to him.
He swam into something glorious
defying breath
as his body
streamline
took to currents
under a crushing weight,
and he found it reassuring.
Seth didn't come up for days.

Then he surfaced with a new outlook.

He crawled over rocks
away from neon tourists lobbing
volleyballs all
distant.

Seth worked to keep the sound of surf
most present.
Avoided hot-dog stands and bumper cars
casinos and the lights of Ferris wheels –
all a blur
from where he camped on the shore alone
making small fires to keep him warm at night
for the first time appreciating heat
and fish, clean-living animals
who leapt above the moonlit ocean
before he swallowed them whole
and dancing.

VII   *Waiting*

What can be written about Isis?
That she went mad?

Her trip was inward where she stood,
feeling the violence of the speeding elements
as she paused in the market place,
or when she traveled by bus to and from
the mundane destinations.

People called her up to know things.
Isis collected Air Miles when she bought her
chardonnay.
Imagined Seth.

All that heat.

The bluest sightless depths and watery graves
sang out through her bones
while the others had no clue.
She had been designed to carry it off.
Built to serve.
People exchanged pleasantries,
inquired after Osiris, her husband.

Her mother's phone words now were long-distance:
"Remember, you are a goddess."

VIII *Sea Change*

Seth camped for many days,
skin tanned
and voice unused
listening only to water.

He thought he might be there forever,
hair growing around him like a house
prepared to witness tides
but not to move.
Then one day as he was dreaming of her laughter
it came to him
rolling in and hidden
in the barrel of a sea chest.
He ran and swept it from the lapping waves,
and carried it like the heart of a loyal friend
to his fire.
His knife sang again

and the lock springs opened.
Seth searched the debris
of someone else's ship-wrecked life
through business cards and serviceable shoes
until he found Book.

Its very bookness made him weep.
He touched it tenderly,
lifted its cover,
as his chest constricted with that new pain
he was learning
to not wish gone.
Words.

He thought of Isis.
How she could dedicate herself to pages
like children,
touching letters with a careful hand.
She had held his knife
not to cut him
but to feel the weight he carried,
and in returning it
had cut herself and bled.
In that split-second Isis winced –
used words to injure
not him
but the idea of injury.
She might have said, "Go away,"
not to him
but to the idea of his absence.
Meant stay.

IX *Seth and Book*

Seth returned with Book
held heavy in his hands.

He had read it on the plane back
oblivious to cloud systems
and landing.
Felt words on his heart
in a sudden language of scar tissue:
muscle built through breakdowns
through poetry.

He did not expect to hate the ending.

Seth had not cheated and read ahead –
he had trusted in the love story completely,
in the sea that kept him
down and green-blind,
held him. A womb.
Floated him to his own fire.

How he hated the ending.

The abolishment of desire
was a foreign language to him.
In the final pages he learned
it was Osiris who would prevail,
transcend
through sacrifice.
What kind of story was that?

Seth walked from the airport
forsaking limos
to her door.
It was night.
She was dressed in white.
He hated that too.

He threw Book at her feet —
spine split and said,
"You knew this?"
Her eyes were the only darkness on her,
almost human.

It was her mouth he kissed
already cool and statue-hard,
the clay tablets going up all over town.
He had been away so long.

X *Seth Discovers He is a Character*

His rejection of the role
played out in the suits he wore.
Seth kept his shoes shined
and found a decent job:
matching socks and a pension plan.
He dropped by on Friday nights
for drinks and casual conversation.
All the time he waited
for something to show on her face
though it never would.

Osiris, too, said he was glad
to see his brother.

While Seth knew the story now
and rage became the way
he breathed
adjusted his tie
removed the cork from her wine
or set a plate on linen,
he did his best to smile back.
Much of him wanted to be the perfect guest
though he could see already
they were parting company.

Lotus flowers erupted in their kitchen.
Sickened him.

He saw Osiris down the hall and mistook him
for a column
then a painted bull
before he came back chuckling.
Isis was growing an outline.
Seth was the only one
casting shadows.

XI *Detachment*

When he killed Osiris
Seth cut the body into fourteen pieces:
eight to pose a question

and six to resolve it.
Death by poetry proved
his chaos had a certain order.
Book, his lover all along, was singing.

XII *What Book Sang*

Isis planted corn near a tamarisk tree,
watched it grow and felt
hawk wings
inside her belly.
Horus would be born and fly
a great god
love-child
of his parents' work:
of death and resurrection
and of chaos, too.

Seth watched. A desert grew . . .

Morning Glories

On my knees in July
I search for morning glory shoots
delicate as babies' wrists
yet capable of killing.
I planted them.

I need to see how they've come up,
where their tightening tendrils coil.

In the bed I check the stems of other plants
for stranglers.
Hunt for leaves like green hearts
and help them find the fence
where they will cling and not destroy.
The fence:
upright constant
marking boundaries,
unable to feel life
but able to bear it.

Veins pulse hidden in the grip of glories,
long to be tended
by a gardener's hands.

How often have I mistaken myself
for wood and wire?

Visitors

My parents visit my garden separately
each searching the foliage
one plant at a time.

I tell them, on their respective walks,
about the season's successes.
How the spring flowers came and went.
How I have planted more from seed this year,
and where the annuals are doing best.

There have been disappointments.
Last fall when I did not know
whether I was staying or leaving this yard
my marriage
I did not plant the tulips.
The dahlia bulbs, unable to winter,
were left in the cold ground.
I have replaced them in new colors.

There is a perennial which none of us can name.
It appears in May in clusters of indigo
flowers connected
each day until July
when the engineering fails.
What makes it different from other plants
is that it vanishes completely before the summer has
gone.

My father advises me
to trim the finished iris stems,
cut back the leaves
for next year.

My mother reminds me
to remove the dry geranium flowers.
This fall, she says, take those plants back to their roots.
Give them rest indoors
so they will thrive again.

The hydrangea reminds us
of our old veranda,
though it's been years
since we three sat there together.

Can't

You can force a horse to water
but you can't force a heart.

You can force a bulb in winter
but you can't force a heart.

Force feed.
Force field.
Gale-force wind.
Brute force.

You can't force a heart.

Her Horses

Her faithful horses drive again,
compact and muscular across her bed
in a small apartment.
Each hoof and flaxen mane
and bare back bore this child
in a spirited chain, unbroken
by what the adults said,
to a new address.
Now they charge
across the parquet plain
well-ribbed and regal,
each one a thoroughbred
with good endurance.
Her commands before sleep
form a soft refrain
each night when she counts them
just to see that no one's fled
in the room with a light
where the gentle beasts reign.
Her faithful horses drive again.

Ghosts

Peonies will fall apart
in the most careful of hands
and leave small, white messages in the grass.
They are ghosts
before the dahlias have bloomed
soft like the skin
of a baby's ear.

I imagine when she looked at him the first time,
loved him instantly and held him,
she did not see how
they were changing
into different forms.

There is a skill to loving through seasons.
Faith in looking through windows
at an empty yard.
Harder than flowers.

Split in the Round

The ripped cocoon and sudden wings begin
unfurling strange against a cast-off shroud.
To live I wear my choices on the wind.

A soul first flutters then beats to dodge the pin.
Once space is glimpsed through broken walls like vows
the ripped cocoon and sudden wings begin.

White world pushed open – and comfort that has been
is changed for different comfort. Rise damaged, proud:
to live I wear my choices on the wind.

Who calls the split in the round a sin
when by design these veins would otherwise be bowed?
The ripped cocoon and sudden wings begin

their flight. In the world that we are in
I have torn myself on my own gate and wept aloud.
To live I wear my choices on the wind.

Release like acid burns my skin
in colors I had only dreamed allowed.
The ripped cocoon and sudden wings begin;
to live I wear my choices on the wind.

Strange Embers

When I swim down to the darkest place
I am surprised by that reel of sudden light:
the shock of bioluminescent travelers.

They dart in currents of their own design,
impossible to follow,
though I have tried.
It's a chemical inside them
that makes them shine
from birth. Purely physical.
Yet I want to attribute their gleam
to the way they glide toward me.
Believe my presence somehow
charges them. Imagine
my eyes lend a reality
otherwise impossible
if I had not swum so far,
so low.

And the water here is crushing me
but I don't notice.

My legs beat giddy in pursuit
of one bright and fleeting form,
strange ember in the deepest recess.
And in that glow a vision heaves –
dying legs and flailing arms.
There is no air or warmth in this show,

only a glimmer of my sunken self.
I wait for them to vanish first
before I surface,
pale and gasping
even for a dull sky.

Keeping Tabs

In bed with essays strewn abroad tonight
she waits to hear the phone, strokes notes in red
on margins, hums, considers what to spread
on a late-night bun. Her thoughts drift off to space.
She muses how that day in the lot their eyes
had locked where lips could not; he said he'd call

and smiled and drove away. She wouldn't call
this wait a thrill, though it's something new tonight
and not a bit like marriage. Alone, she eyes
the clock, folds marking, sighs, and caps her red
Fineliner. Restless, reaches for the space
beneath her bed, that place her stash is spread

for secret comfort. Hauled now on her spread
are tabloid magazines. She will not call
them rags; just keeps them hidden in that space
below what's said. There's no disgrace tonight
in seeking quiet diversion. Letters red
and bold invigorate her tired eyes

that she won't close until her phone rings – eyes
forced wide by a festive cover spread:
Jerk Jilts Her, Jeers, "Kiss Off!" Dumped Dame Sees Red.
And she's aware this waiting some might call
just part of dating irritates tonight.
She'd rather see *Stars' Cellulite* and *Space*

Abductees' Tell-tale Scars. We like our space,
she justifies. Respect each other. Eyes
dart back to *Lies, Lies, Lies!* Tonight
Doll Dukes It Out With Demons: Two-page Spread
On Uptight Dude Caught Dead With Cunning Call
Girl. (Where's the loss and gain in wondering?) Too red,

she thinks, are words sometimes. Reclines, puts red
away. Like that Valentine ungiven, where in the space
below his name she wrote, "with love." Don't call
him now. Don't show you care too much for eyes
that can't be read as plain as letters spread
on newsprint. Then again, what's ever true? Tonight

she curls in blackness, stiffens, shuts her eyes.
The phone rings. Up she bounds, whips back the spread,
spins brightly, "Hey there! Where were you tonight?"

Reality Bites

"You really ought to lighten up," said Vic
at Veg World. "Me, I cleanse myself with beans
when tense, and nuts on sprouts with tempeh, tossed.
The chick peas slay me. Onion soothes all pain
a soul could feel in love. (Undo your jeans
if bloating is a problem, it will pass.)
Those sautéed gold falafel balls may cheer
you up. If jealousy's your thing, gulp greens –
a big fat power shake will get it lost.
Your appetite's still good: Let go, my dear!
Get sauced."

Nymph

You taught me swimming all those summers.
Began by letting me slide
off your back
into the murk.
Stumbled
to clutch at my small shoulders
as you plucked me
clinging and spluttering
my sudden list of injuries.
Scolded:
"Don't be a crybaby.
I didn't let you drown."

That's how I learned to kick.

I called to you as the summers passed
over our wet skin.
Feet toughened by the stones
ran splashing
to perfect my mermaid dives
so you would praise.
You never made it easy.
The ankles had to stay together in the tail.
Body arched stiff
as a shark.
Head disappeared, learned
to navigate in green.

In our lake you could never see the bottom.

Landing was a trick
when the waves were high.
We swam when no one else would
into the breakers
and came out glistening.

It was as if you knew the metaphor already
though you were not much one
for poetry.
You knew what I would need to forgive
even when I was small enough
to ride on your back
and slip
rubbery white
beneath the surface.

You taught me to swim through all conditions.

When it's June I brave the cold great lake.
When the waves roll high
above my head,
dive straight.
Let them hurl me back to shore.
Fall hard and time
the standing up right.

Laugh with water like a lover.

You knew I'd need that mermaid skin,
the tough hide of the nymph.
All those summers,
your last summers,
you made sure we swam each day
and at times when others wouldn't.

Now
at ten on a January night
I push on with wet hair
past the frozen city windows,
return from the pool alone.
I know your gift.
Feel the lengths I've traveled
since you first let me go.

On the Beach with My Daughter

We are collectors on the beach.
We walk with our heads bowed
to small stones and debris
in step
our white bones hidden,
softly moving.

On the shore are fragments
of other travelers.
We bend to lift them from the wet sand,
our fingertips delicately working
while our eyes examine angles
of the end of motion,
light to the touch
and placed
in a child's pail.

Her footprints
and mine
disappearing all the while.

Fabric

When Jazz pulls in on fabric shopping day
we start composed. She's helping me reform
my life and caffeine gives her vision so we
stop on College, four-way flashers on,
and Jazz is gone.

Returns in a frappuccino glaze I've learned
to trust. Now forward thrust on down to Queen
(but not without one thrift shop rove where Jazz
spies macramé she wove in 1975).
Then we arrive

and for a moment I could swear the store
grows hushed. Her fingers brush the first tight bolt
of Chinese orange silk and it falls wide;
that's when I blush and know we'll be a while
in every aisle

all twenty-two. At times there isn't much
to do but follow where this woman's gasps
are heard among the linens, crêpes,
and chintzes, and the toiles – "Oh God, the toiles!"
which she inhales

then strokes, then studies, nods her head and smiles,
"Each one's a story." Jazz's voice is low
when she asks which piece I would have to fill
my home and adds, "Take time and choose with care."
She leaves me there.

I stare at finely printed scenes arrayed
in cottages and streams and children. Pause.
Remember times like these. And here in green
the churning serpent somersaults again,
is not quite slain

though ones with spears eternally stand poised
to strike. I like the blameless cherubs more.
That dog beside the lovers and those geese
seems happy just to be where he is drawn.
There's much to learn

here by the yard, or ponder anyway.
I'd still choose lovers over beasts but here
are both, and minstrels playing under trees,
and tables set with bread and cheese and wine.
This toile is fine . . .

"Fuck, yes!" says Jazz who by this time has torn
apart the store and still wants more to touch.
I'm table-clothed by two, by half-past three
I've got a screen, by four eight pillow shams.
"Excuse me, ma'am,"

a shop clerk scolds, "Please leave the samples on
the hangers." "Oops! I'm sorry yet again,"
says Jazz, more chartreuse hues and dragon flies
to chase, and monkeys bold in fancy hats.
You can't stop that.

My bags are full by five, I'm still alive
and Jazz is pale. We drive in silence now
across the bias seam of city road
tugged back I go to my new fifth-floor home
not quite alone.

A single monkey eyes me through the wrap.
Reminds me of how glad I am that Jazz
can sew. But more, how glad I am for friends
who hug before they go, and drape my world
with grace unfurled.

Lines

I sit with my child
looking at old photographs,
handfuls from a cardboard box
of unsorted life.

We look well organized in two dimensions.
Shadows make lighter forms emerge to tell
an ordered story.
The lines of the past look pre-arranged.
We could not help being who we were,
our contours unavoidable;
old smiles seem definite, kite strings
in the small spring hands of children.

The future does not exist in pictures.
Light and shadow are unknown to it
though sometimes we wish
we could predict its lines.
Lines are infinite,
we say.

In Green

Here in green
by the tangled bed
she stares into branches
that burn her
from the inside.
Outside you do not see
the change yet.

And the sun spins out
its last leafy days.

Ashes
       ashes

invisible as old worlds she knows
but does not write now,
fading.

Instead
sits smouldering
into something new
in a city park
with the cicadas and the fleeting
birds.

And she smiles
as though their wings were hers
sprung hard and sudden
through a weightless skin.

Alive
      alive

determined blooms
in the white heat,
color shot through this ending
like laughter.
Like you, love.

AGMV Marquis
MEMBER OF SCABRINI MEDIA

Quebec, Canada
2002